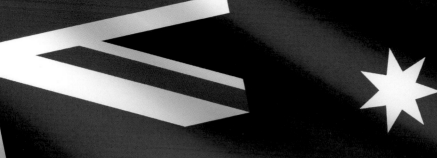

COUNTRY PROFILES

AUSTRALIA

BY MARTY GITLIN

BELLWETHER MEDIA • MINNEAPOLIS, MN

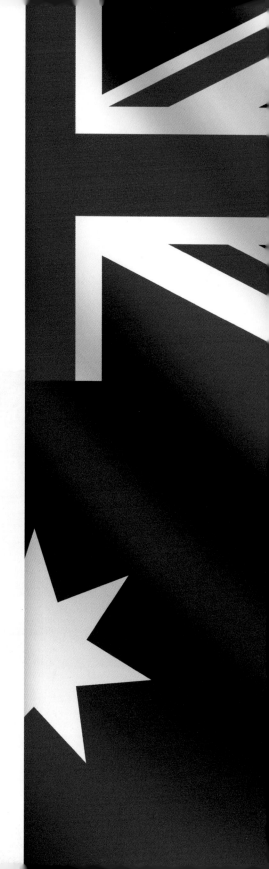

Blastoff! Discovery launches a new mission: reading to learn. Filled with facts and features, each book offers you an exciting new world to explore!

This edition first published in 2018 by Bellwether Media, Inc.

Library of Congress Cataloging-in-Publication Data

Names: Gitlin, Marty, author.
Title: Australia / by Marty Gitlin.
Description: Minneapolis, MN : Bellwether Media, Inc., 2018.
| Series: Blastoff! Discovery: Country Profiles | Includes
bibliographical references and index. | Audience: Grades 3-8.
| Audience: Ages 7-13.
Identifiers: LCCN 2016053595 (print) |
LCCN 2016055670 (ebook) | ISBN
    9781626176751 (hardcover : alkaline paper) | ISBN
    9781681034058 (ebook)
Subjects: LCSH: Australia–Juvenile literature.
Classification: LCC DU96 .G57 2018 (print) | LCC DU96
    (ebook) | DDC 994–dc23
LC record available at https://lccn.loc.gov/2016053595

Editor: Christina Leaf   Designer: Brittany McIntosh

Printed in the United States of America, North Mankato, MN.

TABLE OF CONTENTS

THE AMAZING ROCK   4
LOCATION   6
LANDSCAPE AND CLIMATE   8
WILDLIFE   10
PEOPLE   12
COMMUNITIES   14
CUSTOMS   16
SCHOOL AND WORK   18
PLAY   20
FOOD   22
CELEBRATIONS   24
TIMELINE   26
AUSTRALIA FACTS   28
GLOSSARY   30
TO LEARN MORE   31
INDEX   32

THE AMAZING ROCK

ULURU

An SUV kicks up a cloud of dust as it crosses the open **Outback**. The driver feels a sense of excitement as he spots a massive red stone rising from the earth. It is Uluru, or Ayers Rock. Standing 1,142 feet (348 meters) high and 5.8 miles (9.4 kilometers) around, it is the world's largest **monolith**.

OTHER TOP SITES

GREAT BARRIER REEF

KAKADU NATIONAL PARK

MELBOURNE CRICKET GROUND

SYDNEY OPERA HOUSE

Inside Uluru-Kata Tjuta National Park, the visitor learns about Uluru and its special meaning for the **aboriginal** Anangu people. He hikes to the base of the rock and cranes his neck to take in its size. This is the heart of Australia!

Australia is the only nation in the world that is a continent. The island is also the sixth-largest country in the world. It covers 2,988,902 square miles (7,741,220 square kilometers) and rests between the Indian Ocean and Pacific Ocean. Australia's capital, Canberra, sits in the southeastern part of the country.

Off of Australia's southeastern coast is Tasmania. This island is also part of Australia. The country's closest neighbors include New Zealand, Indonesia, and Papua New Guinea.

INDONESIA

PERTH

INDIAN OCEAN

N
W E
S

PAPUA
NEW GUINEA

AUSTRALIA

▲
ULURU

BRISBANE

SYDNEY

CANBERRA

ADELAIDE

MELBOURNE

PACIFIC
OCEAN

THE CREATURE
FROM A CARTOON

Tasmania is the home of the
Tasmanian devil. Cartoon fans
might know this animal as a
popular Looney Tunes character.

TASMANIA

LANDSCAPE AND CLIMATE

Australia boasts a **diverse** landscape. Forests cover much of the south. In the west, the Outback has huge deserts and dry **scrubland**. Mountains standing in the Great Dividing Range separate the dry interior from **rain forests** along the eastern coast. **Tropical** grasslands cover northern Australia. The **corals** of the Great Barrier Reef spread over thousands of miles along the northeastern coast.

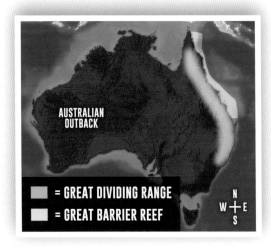

AUSTRALIAN OUTBACK

■ = GREAT DIVIDING RANGE
■ = GREAT BARRIER REEF

N
W ✛ E
S

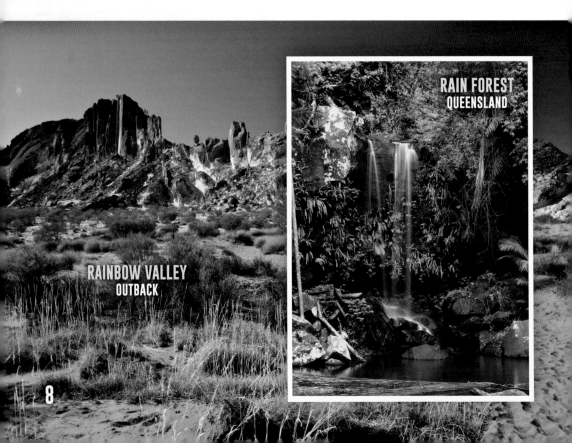

RAINBOW VALLEY
OUTBACK

RAIN FOREST
QUEENSLAND

PULPIT ROCK
GREAT DIVIDING RANGE, NEW SOUTH WALES

CANBERRA

Average seasonal highs and lows

JANUARY
HIGH: 83 °F (28 °C)
LOW: 56 °F (13 °C)

APRIL
HIGH: 69 °F (21 °C)
LOW: 43 °F (6 °C)

JULY
HIGH: 53 °F (12 °C)
LOW: 31 °F (-1 °C)

OCTOBER
HIGH: 68 °F (20 °C)
LOW: 32 °F (0 °C)

°F = degrees Fahrenheit
°C = degrees Celsius

Australians never get too cold. The country is mostly warm and dry. The temperature often soars to 100 degrees Fahrenheit (38 degrees Celsius) in the Outback. Periods of heavy rain occur in the north each summer and in southern Australia in the winter.

Marsupials such as kangaroos and koalas bring Australia quickly to mind. Kangaroos bound across grasslands while koalas make homes in **eucalyptus** forests. Wallabies and wombats are other marsupials that roam the country.

Other exciting and unique animals include duck-billed platypuses. Spiky echidnas wander Australia's deserts and scrublands. In the Outback, wild dogs called dingoes hunt kangaroos and wallabies. Dangerous crocodiles and snakes such as the mainland tiger snake are deadly to animals that get too close. Sea turtles nest and lay eggs on Australia's beaches.

KOALA

ECHIDNA

DINGO

KANGAROO - - - - -

MAINLAND TIGER SNAKE

ODDLY NAMED BIRDS!

Australia is home to many unusually named birds. Among them are laughing kookaburras, sulphur-crested cockatoos, and tawny frogmouths.

- - - - - PLATYPUS

PLATYPUS

Life Span: up to 13 years
Red List Status: near threatened

platypus range = ▪

LEAST CONCERN	NEAR THREATENED	VULNERABLE	ENDANGERED	CRITICALLY ENDANGERED	EXTINCT IN THE WILD	EXTINCT
	▲					

ABORIGINE

The nearly 23 million people that live in Australia are called Australians or Aussies. About one out of every four are British and many others have **ancestors** from Europe. **Immigrants** from Ireland, Italy, Scotland, and Germany have populated Australia. The country has also experienced a growth in immigration from China and other Asian countries. A small number of Australians, called Aborigines, are **native**.

English is the main language for nearly all Australians. No other language is spoken by a significant number of people. Most Australians practice a Christian faith. But many others follow no religion.

FAMOUS FACE
Name: Chris Hemsworth
Birthday: August 11, 1983
Hometown: Melbourne, Australia
Famous for: Stars as Thor in the Marvel superhero movies

SPEAK AUSTRALIAN ENGLISH

ENGLISH	AUSTRALIAN ENGLISH
hello	g'day
great	ripper
well done	good onya
afternoon	arvo
fantastic	beaut
food	tucker
give it a try	give it a burl
everything is fine	she's apples

MELBOURNE

Australians mostly live in houses. The typical house, usually wooden or brick, is one story with a yard. Some city-dwellers live in apartments or townhouses. The average family has one or two kids. Single-parent homes have become more common.

Most Australians live in big cities. Nearly half of the population lives in Sydney, Melbourne, and Brisbane. Many families in cities own cars. But people can also travel by taxi, bus, train, plane, or boat. Communication is no problem for most Australians. Almost all use cell phones. Most homes have Internet connections.

FARMER TECH

Technology is common on Australian farms. Many farmers use the Internet to run their businesses and herd their cattle by helicopter!

CUSTOMS

Australians often greet each other with a friendly "G'day," meaning "hello." They might wave at a friend from a distance, or greet them with a handshake.

Friends sometimes visit each other without notice. However, it is impolite to drop by during mealtimes unless invited. Dinner guests are often treated to a "barbie," or barbecue. They might bring food or a drink for the meal, or the host may provide everything.

BARBIE

TUNING IN TO SCHOOL

Some students in remote areas learn through the School of the Air. It once taught through radio broadcasts. Today it provides lessons through the Internet.

Children in Australia must attend school from ages 6 to 15 or 16, depending on the state. Many extend their education to college. The best universities are found in state capitals. Australian students are required to wear uniforms. Students attending private schools must wear a blazer and hat.

More Aussies work in **service jobs** than any other industry. But Australians have a variety of professions. Farmers raise cattle for beef and sheep for wool, both of which are chief **exports**. Miners gather iron and gold that are also shipped to other countries. Factory workers make valuable products such as steel and automobiles.

FISH MARKET WORKER

SHEEP FARMERS

AUSTRALIAN OPEN

Cricket is the national sport of Australia. It is similar to baseball. Another favorite sport is rugby, a rough game that is much like American football. Australian football is another popular football-type game. Tennis fans enjoy the Australian Open. It is among the biggest tennis events in the world.

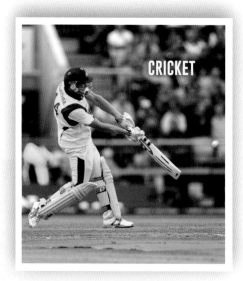

CRICKET

Australians enjoy many outdoor activities. One is a sport similar to basketball called netball, which can also be played indoors. They may also spend time hiking, swimming, surfing, and **snorkeling**.

SNORKELING

BOOGALAH

Boogalah is a game first played by the **Aborigines of New South Wales. It is played with a ball called a boogalah that is made of kangaroo skin. Each team consists of 6 to 10 players.**

What You Need:
- chalk
- rubber ball

How to Play:
1. All the players begin inside a drawn circle.
2. One player throws the boogalah high into the air. The player that catches it moves with their team inside the circle. The other team surrounds them outside the circle.
3. A player inside the circle throws the boogalah high into the air. If a teammate catches it, the team stays in the circle. If the opposing team catches it, the teams switch places.
4. The team that remains in the circle the longest wins the game!

THEY EAT WHAT?

A witchetty grub is a wormy insect common in the Outback. Aborigines may eat them raw or cooked over coals. Others fry the grubs in a pan. Some say they taste like scrambled eggs!

Most Australians eat three meals each day. Some might have "tea," which could be an afternoon snack or evening meal. Table manners are important to many Aussies. It is impolite to place elbows on the table or leave the table before everyone has finished eating.

Australians enjoy many common foods. But they also eat unique Australian foods. Included are the stuffed meat pie and the sausage sanger, which is similar to a hot dog. Australians also favor Vegemite, a salty yeast spread eaten on bread or even pizza. For dessert, Aussies may have a sponge cake known as lamington or a fruit-topped pavlova.

VEGEMITE
LAMINGTON

ANZAC COOKIES RECIPE

Ingredients:
2 cups rolled oats

2 cups flour

2 cups shredded coconut

1 1/2 cups sugar

2 sticks butter

2 tablespoons boiling water

4 tablespoons corn or golden syrup

1 teaspoon baking soda

Steps:
1. Preheat oven to 320 degrees Fahrenheit (160 degrees Celsius). Mix rolled oats, flour, coconut, and sugar in a large mixing bowl.

2. With an adult, melt butter and syrup in a saucepan. Remove from heat.

3. Mix baking soda and water in a cup. Add to melted butter mixture in the pan. Quickly add pan mixture to mixing bowl and stir well.

4. Roll dough into small balls and place on a greased baking tray. Press each lightly with a fork to flatten.

5. Bake for 20 minutes. Remove from oven, let cookies cool, and enjoy!

CELEBRATIONS

Australia celebrates many national holidays. The country's warm temperatures in December lead many to spend Christmas swimming at a beach or pool. On April 25, people honor the Australian armed forces for Anzac Day. The holiday remembers an important battle in World War I. It allows everyone to join together and appreciate the country and its people.

Australia Day is held on January 26. Australians party at home with a barbecue or gather with the community to watch fireworks and parades. They reflect on their past and embrace their future!

AUSTRALIA DAY

ANZAC DAY

1851
Discovery of gold in Australia starts a population boom

1788
The British establish a settlement for criminals in what becomes Sydney

1915
Australian troops fight in the Gallipoli Campaign in World War I, leading to the Anzac Day holiday

1901
Six British colonies, Queensland, New South Wales, Tasmania, South Australia, Victoria, and Western Australia, become the Commonwealth of Australia

1770
British explorer James Cook claims Australia for England

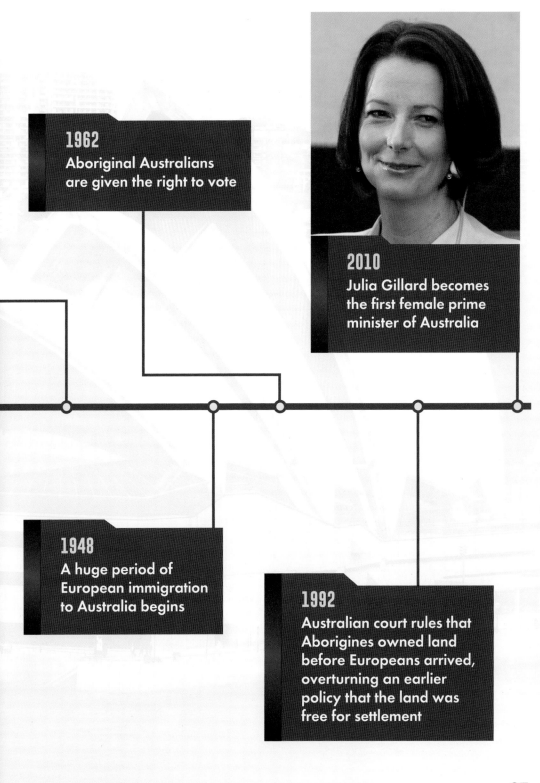

1962
Aboriginal Australians
are given the right to vote

2010
Julia Gillard becomes
the first female prime
minister of Australia

1948
A huge period of
European immigration
to Australia begins

1992
Australian court rules that
Aborigines owned land
before Europeans arrived,
overturning an earlier
policy that the land was
free for settlement

Official Name: Commonwealth of Australia

Flag of Australia: The Australian flag is red, white, and blue. It features a Union Jack symbol on the upper left that shows Australia's link to the United Kingdom. The white star below the Union Jack has seven points to represent the six states and combined territories of Australia. The five white stars on the right stand for the Southern Cross constellation and where Australia sits on a world map.

Area: 2,988,902 square miles
(7,741,220 square kilometers)

Capital City: Canberra

Important Cities: Sydney, Perth, Melbourne, Brisbane, Adelaide

Population:
22,992,654 (July 2016)

COUNTRYSIDE
10.6%

WHERE
PEOPLE LIVE

CITY
89.4%

JOBS

- MANUFACTURING **21.1%**
- FARMING **3.6%**
- SERVICES **75.3%**

Main Exports:

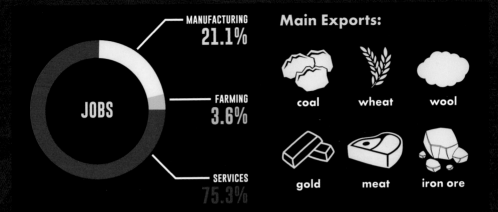

coal · wheat · wool

gold · meat · iron ore

National Holiday:
Australia Day (January 26)

Main Language:
English

Form of Government:
parliamentary democracy

Title for Country Leaders:
prime minister (head of government),
queen (head of state)

RELIGION

- NONE **22.3%**
- OTHER **17%**
- BUDDHIST **2.5%**
- CHRISTIAN **58.2%**

Unit of Money:
Australian dollar; 100 cents equals one dollar.

GLOSSARY

aboriginal—having been in a region from the earliest time

ancestors—relatives who lived long ago

corals—small ocean animals whose skeletons make up coral reefs

diverse—made up of people or things that are different from one another

eucalyptus—a strong-smelling evergreen tree that grows in dry regions

exports—products sold by one country to another

immigrants—people who move to a new country

marsupials—mammals that carry their young in a pouch

monolith—a single block of stone

native—originally from the area or related to a group of people that began in the area

Outback—the large, inland area of Australia where few people live

rain forests—thick, green forests that receive a lot of rain

scrubland—dry land that has mostly low plants and few trees

service jobs—jobs that perform tasks for people or businesses

snorkeling—swimming using a tube to breathe underwater

tropical—part of the tropics; the tropics is a hot, rainy region near the equator.

TO LEARN MORE

AT THE LIBRARY

Blashfield, Jean F. *Australia*. New York, N.Y.: Children's Press, 2012.

Colson, Mary. *Australia*. Chicago, Ill.: Heinemann Library, 2012.

Tieck, Sarah. *Australia*. Minneapolis, Minn.: ABDO Publishing Company, 2014.

ON THE WEB

Learning more about Australia is as easy as 1, 2, 3.

1. Go to www.factsurfer.com.

2. Enter "Australia" into the search box.

3. Click the "Surf" button and you will see a list of related web sites.

With factsurfer.com, finding more information is just a click away.

INDEX

Aborigines, 12, 21, 22
activities, 21
Anzac Day, 24, 25
Australia Day, 24
boogalah (game), 21
Canberra, 6, 7, 9
capital (see Canberra)
celebrations, 24-25
climate, 9
communities, 14-15
customs, 16-17, 22
education, 18
fast facts, 28-29
food, 16, 22-23
Great Barrier Reef, 5, 8
Hemsworth, Chris, 13
housing, 14
landmarks, 4, 5
landscape, 4, 8-9, 10
language, 13
location, 6-7
Outback, 4, 8, 9, 10, 22
people, 5, 12-13
recipe, 23
religion, 13

size, 6
sports, 20, 21
Sydney, 5, 7, 15
Tasmania, 6, 7
timeline, 26-27
transportation, 15
Uluru, 4-5, 7
wildlife, 7, 10-11
work, 15, 19

The images in this book are reproduced through the courtesy of: Aleksandar Todorovic, front cover; Juan Martinez, front cover (flag), pp. 5 (middle top, bottom), 9 (inset), 10 (bottom corner, top), 13 (top, bottom), 14, 19 (top), 23 (top lower), 24-25, 28; Edward Haylan, p. 5 (top); Nils Versemann, p. 5 (middle bottom); Robert Harding/ Alamy Stock Photo, pp. 4-5; Brittany McIntosh, pp. 6-7; Neale Cousland, pp. 8, 20 (top); Mataya/ Getty Images, p. 9; AustralianCamera, p. 8 (inset); worldswildlifewonders, pp. 10-11; Kristian Bell, p. 10 (bottom); Katarina Christenson, p. 11 (inset); FiledIMAGE, p. 10 (middle bottom); Vicki Cain, p. 10 (middle top); Vidler, Steve/ Age Fotostock, p. 12; Nigel Dickinson/ Alamy Stock Photo, p. 15; Aurora Photos/ Alamy Stock Photo, p. 16 (inset); Richard I'Anson/ Getty Images, pp. 16-17; The Sydney Morning Herald/ Contributor/ Getty Images, p. 18; Gary Radler, p. 19 (bottom); Action Plus Sports Images/ Alamy Stock Photo, p. 20 (bottom); Paul Viant/ Getty Images, p. 21 (bottom); ChameleonsEye, p. 21 (top); Suzy Bennett/ Alamy Stock Photo, p. 22 (inset); Andrew Watson/ Getty Images, p. 22; Shane White, p. 23 (bottom); PageSeven, p. 23 (top); Nigel Killeen/ Getty Images, p. 24 (inset); World History Archive/ Alamy Stock Photo, p. 26; ZUMA Press, Inc./ Alamy Stock Photo, p. 27; IID Digital, p. 29 (currency).